NLP

A Beginner's Guide to Neuro-Linguistic Programming

Louise Lowe

Table of Contents

Introduction 1

Chapter 1: The Map 3

Chapter 2: Internal and External Communication 10

Chapter 3: Metamodels 19

Chapter 4: Meta Programs 27

Chapter 5: Making Use of NLP 35

Chapter 6: Presuppositions 42

Chapter 7: Anchoring 50

Conclusion 58

Introduction

There is nothing outside of yourself that can ever save you from who you are. Whether that statement makes you sink into a slum of despair or invigorates you depends entirely on your internal belief system. Despite how content we may be in the different areas of our lives, we all have an idea of who we want to be, who we believe we can be, and what potential we know we have. Time and a lot of resources are often spent looking for a savior of sorts to bridge the gap between where we are and where we want to go. Sometimes it's religion, a dream job, or a relationship. These can all bring immense pleasure and fulfilment to a life, but isn't it strange that even when you "get" whatever it is you thought would fix your life, you keep showing up to sabotage it? If you have already reached the mental place where you know it is you standing in your own way, you have already done half the work. On the other hand, if you are still stuck in blaming other people for how life just seems to keep having a go at you, your narrative is about to change.

In 1976, Richard Bandler, a mathematician who was working as an assistant to linguist John Grinder, decided to create a model of people who had outstanding communication skills. They began by studying three therapists who had varied approaches and different personalities but were all linked by having remarkable success rates with their clients; this is how Neuro-Linguistic Programming (NLP) came to be. Over years of studies, trials, and tests, NLP became a psychological approach for detecting and adapting limiting beliefs and unconscious biases that become barriers to achieving success. Of course, success does not have the same definition for everyone. Needless to say, if your idea of success is a lifetime partner, two kids, and a picket fence, no amount of money or travel can convince you that you have made it in life. As you read this book you will learn that NLP can be used to improve any area of your life. By "improve," I am talking about long-term sustainable growth.

For many goals, there are so-called "easy" fixes, such as with the intention to lose weight. Fad diets and trendy fitness regimes are the most common go-to solutions to drop some unwanted weight, but a tremendous number of people will gain it all back relatively quickly. The reason behind this is that the method used would have worked superficially without actually addressing the root cause of the weight. Psychotherapy generally involves an extensive search to find out why the root is where it is. This often leads to years of therapy because sometimes the individual has no recollection of what really transpired. So, what then? For a lot of people today, spending years going back in time is just not a viable option. Through the use of the NLP techniques that you will find in this book, you can start to see results almost instantaneously. NLP is about looking and moving forward with what has been proven to work. If the plant is not growing well, let's pull it out from the root and plant it where it will inevitably flourish.

The one person who will always be with you, regardless of where you go, is you. So maybe thus far you have been a victim of what you don't know, and what you don't know is that you make choices several times every day to retract, remain, or grow. Fortunately, after this book, you get to decide, now on a conscious level, who you are in the story of your life: a victim of your past or the master of your fate.

Chapter 1: The Map

My perfect summer is not your perfect summer. This idea is particularly apparent in a family where there are children of different age groups. For example, one is in elementary school and the other is in high school. Trying to organize an equally fulfilling day out for the entire family could prove to be a challenge. The parents might be hoping to sunbathe for a while, the one in elementary school would probably rather go back home to get back on their devices, and the high schooler will cringe the whole time, hoping nobody sees them with their parents. They are all experiencing the same summer but their ideas of enjoying it are different. You might rationalize that this is expected according to their ages, and yet would it be correct to assume that every adult would want to spend their summer lying in the sun?

We do this all the time—assume that the way we experience life is the same as the next person, while paying no attention to all the daily situations that show us this just isn't true. Consider what happens after a car accident. People gather around asking what exactly took place. One person might tell you the names of the cars involved in the collision and which driver was in the wrong. Another person might not say or even notice the make of the cars and refer to them based on color. You could also have someone else give you an account of how an elderly man got hit and was rushed to the hospital already. These people were all present and the exact same thing happened before their eyes, but the details they took in were not the same. It comes as no surprise that, after an accident like this, one of the onlookers will leave knowing they will never consider buying a particular car again in their lives, while another may be so badly shaken, they may have nightmares and start avoiding that road. According to NLP, how someone experiences the world individually is their map.

The Map Is Not the Territory

Science tells us that in one second the human mind can potentially be aware of 11 million pieces of information, but only 134,000 of these are absorbed. Everything that is going on around you at any given time is what is referred to as the territory. Based on the example above, the car accident would be part of the territory. You may prefer to look at the territory as what is factually occurring. Everything that was being described by the different individuals was all happening in the territory. Of the 134,000 bits of information that are absorbed, the majority goes into our subconscious mind, and we can only actually track a maximum of less than 50 consciously. What goes into the subconscious will form patterns, linking the new information to similar stored information. This comparison is how we make meaning of what is going on around us, and this meaning is what leads to how we then react, respond, or feel about what happened. This is the map.

The basic assumption of NLP is that the map is not the territory. When the car accident happened, there were also millions of other things going on at the same time; the sun was shining, birds were flying, traffic lights were changing, and people were going about their day also performing their actions. What each person took in at the time depends on who they are as an individual and what meaning they arrived at based on their memories. Before your mind makes the connection and finds meaning in the information, there is no way of knowing how you will feel or react.

This also tells us that our map of the world is a very small and somehow tinted view of reality. We hear and even use the words ourselves often: "I don't know how I missed it. It was right in front of me the whole time." The reason we miss apparent things is that our minds believe the information is irrelevant. You could walk past a cobbler's shop every day without ever being aware of it because your shoes are not broken; it is in the territory but not on your map. So, in essence we see what we are looking for.

While your mind is placing meaning to the data it has taken in, another deciding factor comes into play determining how you will act: how you are feeling in that moment. Teenagers are fully aware of the effects of asking their parents to go to a party on a bad day, so they tactfully wait for the most opportune time, such as when their parents are bubbling and jovial. If we are to take this potential interaction apart, on a day that a parent is feeling stressed, possibly paying the bills, it would be unwise for the teenager to approach them. Their minds have taken in the bills, compared them to all the past bills, and they feel upset. Their map of the world has immediately put up all these walls against anybody who wants to take anything else away from them. This is where the concept of attracting what you hate comes from. In an attempt to avoid, their mind has become a guard on-watch for more predators. Therefore, anything starts looking like a threat. The teenager who is looking for a yes can see that there is none in sight and will retreat until one is on the horizon. Failure to do this will lead to a disappointing interaction for both.

This might seem like a small-scale harmless interaction; however, our lives are built on billions of these that add up to behaviors and attitudes. We are inclined toward the assumption that the world looks the same for all of us and almost resist the possibility that there is another way of looking at the territory that is equally correct and valid. Everything that comes into our conscious mind does so to reaffirm what we believe, filtering out dozens of other essential truths by deletion, distortion, and generalizations.

Deletions

A very easy way of understanding how your mind deletes information is by thinking back to what happens when you peruse a menu in a restaurant. Some people read through everything, some only check out a particular section, and others look for a specific item on the menu. Regardless of which way you do it, you have read through more information than your mind deems necessary. Someone could ask you ten minutes later what was on the menu and you wouldn't have much to say except for the dishes that interested you. How did your mind do this? By deletion. Throughout school, you would have found that the concepts you struggled to retain were from subjects you felt were irrelevant. Everyone could have tried to make you see the importance of geometry but if your mind was made up that this would have nothing to do with your future, the formulas would continue to go right over your head as if you were not in the class.

Deletions assist us in focusing on what needs attention and not getting distracted, but we also miss a lot of useful information. A lot of people get into trouble when Valentine's Day comes, claiming that it slipped their minds. To the offended partner, it may sound absurd, knowing that the entire city morphed into hearts and roses over the past month. While this is probably not the best excuse to provide, it may be entirely true that they did miss all the red because their mind was focused on something else.

Our body works in sync with our minds. If the mind chooses to delete, the mouth will follow suit. This is why the NLP model puts a large emphasis on what you say. Nominalization is a way of saying words that change verbs into nouns. If you have ever had a serious problem with a big company, you probably experienced great frustration at the hands of one person who stood as an obstruction from you reaching the people you thought could help you, using phrases such as "the regulations state" or "management says." These are all skillful deletions of names and ranks. In most cases, nominalizations are an attempt to protect someone. When we say, "the war needs to stop," we are putting out what we feel is safe and deleting information we believe will leave us in a vulnerable position.

Sometimes we use simple deletions in our communications. When someone says, "You're impossible," a whole chunk of information has been deleted. The speaker may assume the other person will understand what they mean, but such deletions allow for sly ambiguity where one can easily switch over and say, "That isn't what I meant." What is important to note is that even if what is said is not a lie, deletions leave out the truth.

Distortions

We like to leave the ability to make up stories to creative writers. You might be surprised to find that your mind is quite colorful, too. One of the ways people frequently distort the truth is by playing "mind reader." How many times have you assumed your co-worker doesn't like you because they don't speak to you? Conversely, how many simple greetings are romanticized because that is how we would rather have seen things? We don't stop at reading minds, though, when it comes to distortions. We also use a technique called "cause and effect" to link two otherwise unrelated aspects. People stay in unhealthy relationships for long periods and even lifetimes because they manage to keep distorting the truth, rationalizing like this: "He is a good father so I can't leave this marriage."

The benefit of being aware of these distortions is that you can begin to challenge ideas you previously accepted as set in stone. It is not only your distortions that you need to take note of, but those of the people you interact with as well. NLP practitioners continue to ask questions when their clients use distortions to help the client reveal to themselves how they have been twisting the truth. When using NLP on yourself, you will take the role of your own practitioner, probing yourself for clarity. The distortions you internalize force you to act according to the story you're telling.

Generalizations

These can be viewed as the stereotypes we see the world through, such as men are dogs and women are emotional. Again, we have a mental collage to back up these claims and we are more willing to attribute what we see to the ready-formed categories than to imagine the possibility of another one. So, we might have consciously rejected these derogatory filters, but what about the not-so-obvious generalizations, like "You're always late" or "Numbers just don't make sense to me." Generalizations might seem easy to detect; however, the way we understand what someone is saying to us is often also through generalizations.

Generalizing allows us to promptly find a category for the information. If you are in an empty parking lot and see an elderly woman, you might feel less threatened because your mind has labeled her as safe. On the other hand, if you see a man who looks homeless, you might decide to move faster because your mind has labeled him as a possible threat. What we label as instinct is sometimes just internal frames of reference sending out alert signals, and to this end, generalizations can be valuable. But, like all other things that protect us from life, they close us to a world of possibilities and opportunities.

The groups that we find ourselves in, some by nature and others by societal categorization, can easily mislead us into thinking we are the same. In reality, we could not be more different, even within these groups. Still, by becoming aware of the smaller categories, we widen our maps and the blinkers fall away.

Chapter 2: Internal and External Communication

The conversation happening inside your body determines what the conversation outside your body means to you. The central nervous system (CNS), which is comprised of the brain and spinal cord, controls the functions of thought, information storage, communication, and reflex actions. Since reflex actions are body reactions that require no thought, this would imply that before our other actions occur, there is a gap for thought regardless of how quickly we respond. What we don't consider in this sequence is all of the unconscious thoughts.

The CNS relies on our five major senses for signals. As the information comes in, the CNS looks around for past experiences as a guide for the best response. Most people find that if they get sick after having eaten a certain food, the next time they encounter it, they immediately feel repulsed. This doesn't mean that if they ate an old piece of pie the last time, the next one would also be stale. However, the most recent information with the most powerful reaction has their mind believing that pies are a threat and will react to this effect.

If there is no past information to go on, the mind will do something slightly more fascinating. It will go far back to look for solutions from the formative years of your life. Ultimately, it will boil down to your mind's perception of the received signals, and this is why two people react differently to the very same situation.

Communication Modalities and Representational Systems

In NLP, our five senses symbolize our individual representational systems. Everyone has a primary representational system, and you can determine your own by asking yourself what your preferred way of receiving information is. Alternatively, you could also pay attention to your word choice (predicates) to guide you. According to the Visual, Auditory, Kinesthetic, Olfactory, or Gustatory (VAKOG) System, you have predominant communication modalities, encompassing both internal (within our body) and external (with other people) communication.

Visual

Visual individuals find it easier to understand and remember things that they see happening. Out of habit these days, most people will opt to watch a video about something rather than to read or attend a lecture about it. However, after simply watching, a visual person will have retained more information than any of the other types of people. When they need to refer to the information again, they are easily able to replay what they saw in their minds. They are also more likely to be able to tell you what the speaker looked like and the clothing they wore and will take notice of the smallest visual details. By choice, visual people will be drawn toward careers and hobbies that allow them to use their sense of vision.

When visual people speak, they tend to speak fast, which is associated with the need to verbally meet the speed of the pictures in their minds. They regularly use the following phrases, which all indicate how their internal representational system works:

- It appears to me that...
- Look at it this way.
- I don't see how...
- We will see how it goes.

Auditory

If you can easily recall the exact words someone said, you could be an auditory person. This group of people are not only great listeners, but they will also often mirror what you have said. They do this in order to process what is being said. Auditory people are also very sensitive to sound, so if they are trying to concentrate, random or loud sounds will irritate them more than the other groups. They will even tell you that they cannot hear their thoughts when music is too loud. Unlike the visual person, the auditory person does not need to see something happening for it to make sense to them; they do, though, require a verbal explanation to go on.

To spot an auditory person, lookout for the ones who get fully engrossed in a conversation. They will describe through an auditory lens and might use the following phrases:

- I hear you.
- Let's discuss that.
- This doesn't sound right.
- Sounds good to me.

Kinesthetic

Kinesthetic individuals need to do things for them to make sense. They dislike being forced to sit still for long periods, listen to someone speak, or watch something happen. Likewise, trying to get them to understand something they haven't actively partaken in is rarely a success. Kinesthetic people are usually of high emotional intelligence. They only make up approximately 5% of the population. They would preferably work in environments where they get to move around and multitask. If you are trying to identify them through speech, lookout for words that relate to physical sensations and actions, such as the following:

- Something doesn't feel right.
- I'm not following you.
- Let's start again from scratch.
- Don't pressure me.

Olfactory and Gustatory

Visual, auditory, and kinesthetic are considered the most probable representational systems that individuals will have. Olfactory and gustatory are more secondary and can be used to enhance experiences for both personal uses and when communicating with other people. An individual who has a strong olfactory representational system will often make use of their sense of smell. When speaking about a past event, they will tell you how they could smell flowers or food. A gustatory person will recall tastes.

Knowing yourself is pivotal to your success. If you are a visual learner who has been trying to excel in an auditory-based environment, it can take twice as much time to learn what an auditory person would. With this knowledge, you can begin to carve your world to suit your primary representational system. As you read further, you will also see how knowledge of other people's representational systems can make communication less awkward.

Eye Accessing Cues

You may have figured out your representational system, but it might not be as easy to know that of the next person without asking invasive questions. Eye accessing cues are another way of finding out an individual's representational system as well as other indicators in communication that are valuable. It is often said that eyes are the windows to the soul; your eyes work in connection to the parts of your brain in use at the time. The eye accessing cues show signs for visual, auditory, and kinesthetic thought.

The eye accessing cues are based on what is called a normally organized pattern. Those who do not follow the rules of this pattern are categorized as reverse organized.

Visual Construction

When a person is forming visual images in their minds, they will often look up and to the left. So, if a visual person is lying, this is where their eyes will go. However, if you are to ask a visual person for an example of what their dream house would look like, they would not necessarily be lying but will look up and to the left as they construct the images of their house mentally.

Visual Recall/ Remembering

If you ask an individual with a normally organized pattern what they ate for dinner four nights ago, they will probably look up and to the right as they try to visualize the plate that was in front of them. If they look to the left instead, this could imply that they are making up a story about what they ate.

Auditory Construct

Auditory construction (when an auditory-dominant person is mentally creating) is reflected as the eyes look directly to the left. This can be brought about by questions or making requests that make an individual think of what they plan to say or hear in the future. You could say to a person, "If you had an opportunity to speak to your late grandparent again, what would you say?" A left glance would be expected.

Auditory Recall/ Remembering

When bringing back to mind a conversation that already occurred, this would be an auditory recall and the expected eye cue would be a direct look to the right. If someone simply has a reason to remember a past event but looks to the left, this would suggest that they are recalling conversations and sounds from that event. This would bring us to assume the individual has an auditory representational system.

Kinesthetic Thought

At times, when a person who has a normally organized pattern is concentrating on physical or emotional feelings, their eye movement will be down and toward the left. This is directly opposite to auditory digital thought, where the look would also go down but to the right, indicating internal dialogue.

People tend to look directly ahead with no eye movement when they are being truthful and therefore relying on information naturally. Although many people are aware of eye accessing cues, they have limited control over their representational systems. You can use this to your advantage, knowing whether you have established rapport and how to proceed with an interaction.

Rapport

Before you can effectively communicate with another person, it is crucial to begin by building rapport. Rapport refers to the establishment of a relationship of trust before proceeding to the intention of the interaction. Communication is an essential part of NLP because it takes up such a large part of our lives and has more effects than we are aware of. Most people think of building rapport in terms of sales and counseling sessions. These are two examples of how rapport makes all the difference; however, we often fail to achieve fruitful communication with the people in our lives because we don't bother to first, level with them.

The idea behind building rapport is, during that moment, you intentionally stop seeing the world from your own perspective and try to cross over and understand the other person's view. Like all other positive reactions, this then opens them up to the possibility of also seeing things from your point of view. Without rapport, everyone is just basically walking around self-absorbed. The classic example has always been of one partner getting home from a long day at work. They have spent hours dealing with clients and colleagues, maybe a boss, too, and all they want to do is sit in silence and have a decent meal. The partner who was at home has been busy themselves, lonely, and has been looking forward to having some adult interaction at the end of the day. Their optimism is crushed by the demeanor of the person who walks in through the door. The rest of the night is ruined; no one was able to cross over into the other one's perspective.

Genuine building of rapport cannot be faked—you need to be fully attentive to the person you want to have a conversation with, taking in their entire physiological behavior. The first thing you would want to do in building rapport is to find similarities between you and the individual, such as ethnicity, age group, or gender. People are generally more receptive to people with whom they share similarities. The catch is to aim for correspondence in aspects you would not have to verbally highlight. If this cannot be found, you can move on to creating similarity by mirroring the person's body language, which is where the eye accessing cues become useful. They can help you develop a real connection with the person you are talking to, because after all, aren't we all hoping to find people who understand us? Mirroring includes breathing rate, voice projection, tone, and pace. Asking questions lets a person know that you are actually interested in what they are talking about. However, people generally find it tedious and unpleasant when someone speaks about themselves at length. If you begin a conversation by asking one question after the other, without divulging any information about yourself as well, the communication takes on the air of interrogation, which can ultimately cause the other party to pull away from you.

Chapter 3: Metamodels

Knowing that we cut out useful information from our maps of the world through deletions, distortions, and generalizations, metamodeling is a concept of questions designed specifically to challenge that map. Language puts our internal mental state into words and is, therefore, a gateway into understanding what limitations you or another person may have. Metamodels take into consideration two structures in every person: the surface structure and the deep structure. The surface structure is where we see the information being cut out from the experience, for example when someone says, "Everyone at work hates me." This is how they are seeing the world; however, it does not mean that what they are saying is true. An NLP practitioner in this instance could ask the following questions: "Do you mean every single person at your workplace?" or "How do you know they hate you?" The answers to these questions serve the purpose of expanding the speaker's map of their work environment.

The following section will address common metamodel patterns and show you questions you can begin to ask yourself and others. Understand that you have been operating on these models for an extended period, so creating a new way of thinking will take time, practice, and repetition.

Assumptions

As humans, we tend to be slightly arrogant in our thoughts. We may not necessarily use the words "I know" in our statements but we make multitudes of assumptions. Our assumptions can help us in being more productive, yet they can also give us excuses for complacency, such as "I would have to be taller to make it in basketball." The clear assumption is that, for a person to be successful in basketball, they need to be at least a certain height. There is, however, also a hidden assumption: that you are skilled and the only thing stopping you is that you are not tall. The resulting pattern of thought will likely be that there is no point in trying, particularly if you are past the age of growing much taller. This situation could be instantly expanded by asking the question "How do you know that you would have made it?" or "How do you know you need to be tall to make it in basketball?"

Complex Equivalence Patterns

By monitoring our speech, we can also pick up where we make similarities between two different experiences and phenomena without a factual basis, which is called complex equivalence. Take the example "My client just pulled out of the deal. This is going to be a bad day." A client's withdrawal from an agreement you had been working on will inevitably put a dampener on your mood, but this does not correlate with how the rest of the day will go. Rather, you would have made a decision there and then to have a horrible day, and of course, everything that comes into your map for the duration of your day will comply. You might believe that in such a scenario you would not have the presence of mind to ask yourself questions that challenge your perspective, but this is also a story you are telling yourself. Until you tell yourself a different story, you will continue to be led by old patterns. Once you make statements of complex equivalence, ask yourself, "How did I come to this conclusion?"

Lost Performative

Think about the following sentence: "You will waste a lot of time trying to multitask." This is an example of a lost performative, which is a factual claim made without the backing of a source or evidence. Possibly the person who is having this thought or saying these words may have been unsuccessful at an attempt to multitask. What this then highlights, is how often we assume that a couple of failures equate to impossibility. When we have decided this is the truth for us, we then expect it to be the truth for other people. Challenge the idea by asking, "According to whom?"

Unspecified Verbs and Nouns

When a verb or noun is unspecified in a sentence, it is said in a way that does not give you enough information, thereby leaving a substantial amount of room for imagination. When someone says, "their children lack discipline," the only part of the sentence that is clear is the subject: children. The verb "lack" indicates the absence of something, however, it does not specify to what extent. "Discipline," as a noun, can mean one thing to the speaker and something else to the listener. When you unintentionally form sentences like this, step back and ask yourself what exactly you are avoiding saying. By making a habit out of speaking this way, we are choosing to bring fog into an otherwise clear situation. One sure way to pick out unspecified verbs and nouns is by assessing whether you can easily visualize what you just said or thought, without the background knowledge. Unspecified verbs and nouns are generally easier to identify in another person's speech, but with commitment, you will be able to stop yourself and become more articulate.

The Milton Model

The Milton Model operates almost in opposition to metamodels, as it requires the very ambiguity that metamodels avoid. When using the Milton Model, the intention is to speak in a way that matches the natural unconscious mind, making it easier to get someone to agree with you, so you would use this model more effectively in outer communication. The Milton Model makes use of all the metamodels above with intention. For example, you may use "I know" statements to encourage a particular line of thought in someone, like "I know you are tired of viewing more houses and I would like to help you to find what you are looking for." The way this is phrased validates emotions that a client would not have expressed yet but would make perfect sense. By using the word "and" instead of "but," you do not sound contradictory or inconsiderate of the client's position. Hypnotists and guided meditations make use of the Milton Model to increase suggestibility in their clients, such as "As you exhale, your body will begin to relax."

Modal Operators

Modal operators are indicators in a person's speech of what motivates them. People generally operate in six modes: necessity, negative necessity, possibility, impossibility, desire, or choice. These modes affect the overall experience of a person's life or may be area specific. Modal operators fall into the category of generalizations.

Necessity and Negative Necessity

When we use words such as "must", "should," "shouldn't," or "cannot," it shows that in our maps we believe there is no choice with regard to what is to be done. Not having a choice creates an environment of perceived stress. Stress is not always a bad thing; sometimes the pressure of meeting a deadline leads us to be more productive and focused on our work. When stress becomes the way of life, then it becomes unhealthy. Taking notice of modal operators of necessity and negative necessity can define areas of your life that are unnecessarily cluttered. Let's use the morning as an example. You believe you should have gotten your eight hours of sleep to operate optimally, you should meditate and exercise early, the kids must eat before school, and they mustn't get to school late. If you are working on the same clock that the rest of the world is working on, this is most likely a very stressful morning and will continue to be without conscious changes. By all means, getting the children to school on time would be a priority that will come with complications if not met. However, other beliefs might be more flexible, such as the amount of sleep you require to function well or the time of day you meditate or exercise.

When a necessity mindset creeps into other areas of our life, we may find ourselves living based on limiting beliefs, like "I must stay at this job for at least five years" or "I can't quit sugar." If you say these words enough times, you will believe them, and it becomes a self-fulfilling prophecy. Listening to our own speech is not always easy, but to find where you operate in necessity, you could start with aspects of your day or your life that make you feel pressured or unhappy.

Possibility and Impossibility

We all have a list, long or short, of impossibilities, meaning things we do not do, people we do not speak to, or places we do not go. Right now, it is probably still a mental list but find time to try and write out as many as you can. It can be food, jobs, and even conversations we move away from whenever they start. As you list them, you might even feel your body begin to tense, which is a natural defensive response. The good thing is that in this exercise you do not have to defend your impossibilities to anyone but yourself. Now, ask yourself, item by item, "Why not?" Let's assume you find the impossibility "I don't forgive easily" on your list. Your initial reason could be "People take me for granted when I do." Which people would this be and how did you come to this conclusion? Has one or a few unpleasant experiences led you to live an unforgiving life?

A modal operator of possibility opens you up to many other possibilities. When you speak from the point of view of being able to do and at least try, your mind and body are willing to support with action.

Desire

So, what is it that you truly want? Most people struggle with this question. Firstly, because from a very young age, we are taught that "want does not get." It is so ingrained in our thought patterns that even as adults we continue to feel guilty about desiring. Occasionally, those who are bold enough to answer this question might decide to use words that justify their desires, like "I just want a decent salary" or "All I'm asking for is good health." Once again, the words are reflecting an internal environment where the individual feels they should not desire more. Desire is a necessary motivator to moving from a position of stagnation. If you refuse to desire, your mind has no reason toward meeting your goal. Begin to speak to yourself with clarity, and then do the same with other people. For example, try saying "I want to ace my next project" or "I want to understand you." Then, write another list of the things you desire.

Choice

Now, go through both lists again and ask two questions for each item: "What is stopping me from doing this?" and "What would happen if I did?" You might find things you do not wish to change from the first list, like "I avoid eating avocados because they feel slimy in my mouth." What is different now is that you know that it isn't impossible for you to eat one and possibly if that was the only food on an island you were stuck on, you would. You might also find that there are links between the list of impossibilities and the list of desires. For example, "I do not date short men" could be on list one and "I want a stable relationship" could be on list two. By comparing the two, you can see an instant reduction of your map, which is unlikely to have a sound basis. Now that you are fully aware that this is a choice you are making, you are the author of your life.

Chapter 4: Meta Programs

Self-mastery will always begin with self-discovery. You are the best person to get to know yourself because many things go on inside your mind that you will never directly verbalize, some by choice. If you are focused, reflective, and attentive, you will notice the patterns and find where your mental roads suddenly take a turn and where barriers are instantly dropped, seemingly out of nowhere, to stop you from going ahead. Meta programs are these unconscious patterns we are running on, like computers. So basically, the computer is not dead, but is it running on a suitable program? Maybe it needs an upgrade or possibly the system is infected with viruses. Except, we do this with our computers, don't we? Notice a glitch, get irritated by it once or twice, and then get used to it until we don't notice the malfunction anymore. It might take someone else attempting to use our computer to bring it to light, and still, we could just shrug it off and think "Ah well, it isn't theirs to have a problem with." Using a poorly functioning computer will cost you time, opportunities, information, and scope. In case you don't know where the glitches in your system are, meta programs show you a categorized system alert.

Internal or External Frame of Reference

Your frame of reference is where or who you look to for decision-making. A person with an internal frame of reference will trust their own opinion. They will not rely on other people to feel good about themselves or to use as a yardstick for success. In a workspace, these will also be the individuals who prefer to work alone, only requiring clearly set out targets to get going. The flipside of an internal frame of reference can present as a very self-absorbed person with total disregard of other people and their desires. On the other hand, a person with an external frame of reference makes their decisions based on what other people think, do, or tell them. They want feedback, reassurance, and will gravitate toward group work for confidence. In excess, an external frame of reference will result in a life that they did not genuinely desire, such as having the job their parents wanted them to have, the car their friends think is cool, and the partner they were told would be an asset.

Your frame of reference will undoubtedly have roots in your upbringing. Most children with an internal frame are quickly labeled as being stubborn or maybe more courteously as strong-willed. The way life plays out, moving away from home and making your meals, encourages those who have an external frame of reference to begin to make their own decisions. But this does not always happen. Many cultures and religions around the world teach female members of society to turn to males for decisions. As a result, the women raised in these societies back away from decision-making, and the men charge ahead without considering the women's opinions. Forcefully breaking away from these societal ties can likewise lead to arrogant women and indecisive men.

Balance is the key to a healthy frame of reference, internalizing when making decisions about your own life and preferences and externalizing to learn about and understand other people's experience of the world as well.

Toward or Away

When you see something and you want it, what is your usual action? For someone who has a toward pattern, the reaction will be to immediately go for it. Many decisions we encounter will require an immediate yes in everyday conversations, such as a colleague planning a weekend get-together on a whim, who asks, "Are you in?" It could also be a time-sensitive job opportunity. Believe it or not, many people move away from the things they desire. We can use all types of excuses to justify why we do so: needing to speak to someone else about it, requiring time to think it through, or the idea that "what is mine will never miss me." All these beliefs are valid and can actually be evidence of balance and making sure you make a level-headed decision, but the truth is most people often already know the truth. You already know when you take a pause, whether you are going to look for a backup to your "yes" or your "no."

Once you know that your running program is to blindly rush ahead, you can learn to wait and ensure you genuinely want something before proceeding. The more spontaneous acts you regret, the less you can trust yourself. Conversely, if you consistently talk yourself out of what you want, change your course of action to looking for affirmations to go forward. Start with small things, like trying a new hobby. As you gain confidence, ask yourself what the worst-case scenario would be. Chances are it won't be a train wreck.

Sorting By Self or By Others

Sorting by self or sorting by others meta programs usually run concurrently with the internal and external frames of reference, respectively. An individual who sorts by self is reluctant and resists anything that doesn't benefit them directly. Sometimes a person will have an external frame of reference, but sort by self. They will come across as very selfish but strangely always looking for other people's approval and admiration. The opposite, which is a person with an internal frame of reference while sorting by others, will reflect as someone who doesn't need external motivation to help other people, so there is some balance there, but these people can also appear as being controlling because, without consulting anyone, they decide what is best for others.

Being selfish is one of the hardest traits to pick up in yourself because there is a story holding the actions intact. It would be easier to ask yourself when the last time was that you did something for another person that had no benefit, at all, to you. Equally, you could ask yourself when you last did something advantageous to you. If you are patterned to keep doing things that are beneficial to others at the cost of your well-being, you will burn out. Burnout doesn't change patterns of behavior, though; it simply leads to a resentful mindset.

Convincer

This meta program is about what influences you when you decide to do or not do something. Automatic convincers are trusting to a level of gullibility; they believe whatever they are told. Knowing the number of unethical transactions in the world, it is easy to see why being an automatic convincer would come with unnecessary risk. Other people require statistics or time lapses to be convinced. These are both reasonable ways of looking for justification before acting. However, flexibility is key, as not all statistics are true and sometimes ten years of experience does not amount to skill. Never convincers are exactly that—there is nothing you can do to convince them of your worth. If you are dealing with a never convincer, this knowledge might better be used to save yourself the time of trying to convince them. To know your convincer program, look around yourself for something you may have initially been hesitant to buy into, and ask "what did it take to convince you?" To know another person's convincer program, ask questions relating to the same.

Matcher Versus Mismatcher

Is there this one person who you almost always know will kick up a fuss about anything? Those people who will always go against the tide? Or is this person you? Mismatchers do not want what everyone else wants. They are not looking to create harmony in any form. When you are working in a team, it is usually helpful to have at least one person who sees things from a different perspective, as this can cover blind spots. It becomes a nightmare, though, when they become antagonistic and slow everyone else down just for the sake of being different. Matchers do the opposite; they stay in line with everyone else. They do not like to rock the boat. In excess, matchers get out of touch with their own ideas and seem pretentious.

Time Sort

Mindfulness has only grown in popularity recently because people are becoming more aware that they escape the present often. We all have past attachments and memories we may think and talk about sometimes. This is different from a person who refers to the past frequently. They might consciously know that they cannot return to the past, whether to enjoy it or to resolve it, but their subconscious mind continues to get signals of wanting to go back. This can result in an unexplained stagnation in the person's life. Goals are an important part of NLP, specifically setting them clearly and allowing your mind to lead you to them. By advising people to stay focused on their goals, a misconception forms that they must live in the future. For your dreams to become realities, you would need to return to the present to pave the way to the future.

Negative or Positive

A series of unfavorable events can lead someone to have a pessimistic outlook; it doesn't have to have been catastrophic, just emotionally linked enough to pour gray all over their lens. Of course, growing up in a negative environment can also make pessimism look normal, safer, and even humble in some societies. A person with a positive mindset expects life to work out for them. They are aware that things won't always turn out the way you might want them to, but their positivity draws their focus to the bright side of things. While being optimistic is a more fruitful pattern to have, misplaced optimism can be upsetting. Few people want to hear that there's a positive side when they are bereaved. The negative or positive meta programs are classic examples of how the mind will find what it is looking for.

Reframing

Once you have been able to find the programs' operation, you can decide to change them. Again, your decision to change or continue working with a glitch will depend on your meta programs. Knowing now that the meaning of something communicated is the response received, it tells us that your actions are based on how you are translating occurrences. Reframing is a way of changing the meaning of your outer world for you to act differently, as you would like to.

One way you can change your point of view is by context reframing. To do this, you start by selecting a behavior you are not happy with. Let's go with people-pleasing. You could have an external frame of reference, such as waiting on people's smiles to feel like you have done a good job. This is exhausting, but in a different context, you would make an incredible host. The behavior is not bad—it just needs to be used in the appropriate setting.

Another way you can reframe is content reframing. For example, consider being self-absorbed. You have an internal frame of reference and are quite oblivious to other people's opinions. From a social point of view, evidently, this would be problematic, but what is the intention behind being self-absorbed? Possibly you avoid being derailed from your goal. Having found the positive intention behind your withdrawal from other people, you can explore other ways of staying focused or communicating this effectively to the people around you.

Other than a conscious decision, the only other way that a person's meta programs change is by experiencing an emotional event of significance. Most of these events are traumatic, and you will hear people say they were never the same again after the experience. Others will call it a moment of enlightenment, but what this all means is simply that their view of the world has changed, so they cannot behave the way they once did.

Chapter 5: Making Use of NLP

As you begin to know yourself better and understand your patterns, you will want to start using NLP actively. To avoid being overwhelmed, you can choose to focus on one area of your life at a time, but you will soon notice that you automatically begin to adopt a new outlook on life that will seep into all areas without as much effort.

NLP in the Workplace

Several NLP principles can be used to improve and maximize our careers. You could start by determining whether you have the job you truly want. This takes into consideration how you wound up with the job you have—it could have been out of your circumstances or maybe you were advised to take up that job. After a certain number of years, people tend to settle for the jobs they have. If you choose to do so, you can reframe your decision to allow yourself to enjoy your working environment. Instead of saying "I have to work here because this is the only job I could get," you could choose to dwell on the idea that "This is the job that allows me to earn a salary, and I am grateful for the opportunity."

Depending on the type of job you have, the use of NLP would encourage being bold and going outside of the box, which are traits that are suitable for creative careers, as well as those that frequently require finding solutions. Knowing how to listen to more than the words clients and customers use, improves your service and efficiency. Companies around the world incorporate

NLP techniques into sales to build better and more fruitful connections for both parties involved. They are migrating from the idea of prioritizing only the happiness of the clients to also ensuring their employees are content.

The use of NLP also helps you to be more accommodative of other personalities, where previously you may have judged your colleagues for their quirks and behaviors contradictory to your own. Instead of looking at their actions on the surface, you know that you could not possibly know what is going on in another's world. With the knowledge of how your feelings have an effect on how you react, it stops making sense to spend time complaining about a workmate's behavior as this only makes you more irritable and has no positive effect on their actions.

Social Life

It's not news that while technology has made it easier for people to keep in touch, authentic connections have become rarer. Having a large following on social media doesn't satisfy the natural human desire for social interaction. You can start by defining what you would like your social life to look like; this could be having more friends or being invited to social events. Ask yourself what is standing in the way of you having what you want.

Social anxiety is a condition where an individual finds social interactions uncomfortable. The level to which this will affect people will differ. For some, it is any social communication, while for others, having to speak in front of people paralyzes them. People who struggle with social anxiety will turn down opportunities and find excuses to avoid events. Social anxiety is a medical condition, and NLP cannot replace the treatment. Where the anxiety is only tied to specific occurrences, like making a presentation, two NLP techniques can be utilized to break past this barrier: the Fast Phobia Process and the Swish Pattern.

Phobias develop from being over-associated with a past event. Association with an event means that when you recall what happened, you feel like you are reliving the experience. With disassociation, the memory plays in your mind, as if you are watching yourself. In most cases, you will have some memories that are disassociated and others that are associated. The Fast Phobia Process is an NLP technique designed for you to disassociate from traumatic events.

To complete the Fast Phobia Process, you need to find yourself a quiet place where you will be undisturbed. Recall the event that triggers anxiety for you, and then close your eyes and imagine you are in a cinema, sitting right in the middle with the screen ahead. Now, see on the screen the event paused, in black and white; maybe it was a time you stood in front of an audience and forgot the words you had planned to say. You then need to find a three-point disassociation, and you do this by imagining yourself floating away from your body to the projection booth so that you can see both the black and white movie, and yourself sitting in the theater. Watch the movie from the perspective of a disassociated observer. When the movie ends, watch it again but in reverse, slowly. If you keep replaying the movie backward, a minimum of at least ten times, the sensations that trigger the anxiety will begin to fade until recalling the event does not make you anxious anymore.

Another way of dealing with anxiety is using the Swish Pattern. With this method, you begin by finding the trigger for the anxiety as well. Try and remember what exactly happens immediately before the anxiety kicks in; it could be seeing multiple eyes focused on you. Take a mental picture of this and hold the image. Now, create another picture in your mind. This time make it one of how you would like to behave: the confidence you would like to exude and the calmness you would have in order to speak with clarity. Now that you have two pictures in your mind, take the trigger picture and make it bold and larger in your mind, while simultaneously shrinking the preferred picture into a small, dark picture on the left side of your mind. Hold the pictures as they are for a moment, then make a rapid switch (swish) replacing each picture with the other, so now the preferred picture is the enlarged one and the trigger is tiny. Repeat this as many times as you need to, and eventually, you will stop feeling triggered by the first image.

Both the Fast Phobia and the Swish Processes can be used for other troubling behaviors that stop you from living a full life. They have been successfully used for snake and flight phobias, as well as for smoking and other addictions.

Relationships

Fairy tales have definitely caused chaos in terms of relational expectations, but so has the idea of finding someone who will "just get you." Based on the fundamental aspects of NLP, we are able to understand why this is an unrealistic and unfair burden to expect another person to carry. Regardless of how well you may believe you know someone, there is so much more you do not know, simply because we are complex beings. Your relationships cannot be fulfilling if you hold onto patterns and goals that are elusive. If you do not already have a partner and desire one, you could begin by being more intentional. NLP practitioners will tell you that an unbelievable number of clients will resist being intentional about their relationships because they are completely sold on the idea of chance encounters. Needless to say, all roads lead back to Hollywood. What relationship frame persists in your mind, and who put it there?

The idea that great relationships require no effort stops us from realizing the ability we have to build something meaningful with another person. As is the case in other areas of your life, you would need to have an overall goal for what you want your relationship to be and then cut it down into smaller short-term goals. The communication in your relationship could completely change by setting goals for how you would like to interact with your partner, following through by being intentional with your speech and body language. You could set a goal that you are going to give your partner the attention they ask for, set aside time for them, and give them undivided focus.

At any point in your relationship, you can decide to set a goal and redirect from where you have been and where you were headed. The reason behind this is that most people set the goal to be with a person, get them to date you, have them commit to you, move in together, or get married, but they have no sense of direction for where the relationship should go after that. If you look at your partner from a curious perspective, you will realize that there is a gold mine in them, just as there is in yourself.

When you hear someone in a relationship say, "a relationship is a two-way street," they believe they have done their part and the onus is on the other person to meet them where they are. Possibly, you make a conscious decision that you do not want to fight with your partner. You get home and only respond when necessary or when spoken to. Your silence had a positive intention, but now you know that the meaning of your communication is the response you get. To your partner, your silence may mean a lack of effort or interest in them. Isn't it interesting the amount of time we waste trying to change everyone else except the one person that we do have the power and ability to change?

Because of our differences, there will inevitably be behaviors your partner has that you will find disturbing. Instead of magnifying the behavior, you can reframe it by identifying the positive intention behind their actions, such as taking their tendency to complain and framing it as a sign that they still want to be with you and improve the relationship. Not complaining could be a sign of giving up.

Good Habits, Good Life

Goals are meant to be used as indicators—not as finalities. Change becomes difficult to sustain when the focus is on a goal and not a state of being. We see this all the time with people who win the lottery before their minds think in terms of abundance; they lose the money rapidly because they remain who they were before they had millions. The only person blocking you from becoming the you of your dreams is the stubborn, outdated model who keeps talking you out of an upgrade. Take some time to explore who you want to be. This is the point where most people get lost, focusing on external elements, like wealth, a sculpted body, or a lifestyle. These may be products of who you become, but who you want to be is about the traits you want to possess and the map you want to have of the world.

As you go through the traits you desire, question why each one is important to you. If we take the trait of being knowledgeable, this could be important to you because learning more increases your awareness and sparks your creativity. If you are to find that being knowledgeable only made the list because someone told you it was important to be so, you may just as well scratch it off and leave it out until it has an intrinsic value to you. Once you have completed your description, compare this version of yourself to who you are now, taking note of the areas that need modification. Now you can determine what habits and routines you would need in place to become the desired version of yourself. Most likely, you will find that the new habits you would have to form will contradict the ones you have at present, meaning the old habits are now undesirable habits to you. The Swish Pattern works effectively in replacing these old habits with the new.

There is always the question of how long it takes before an action becomes a habit. Timelines range between one to nine months, with 66 days being the average. The more compelling your desired identity is to you, the easier it will be for you to remain committed.

Chapter 6: Presuppositions

NLP presuppositions are a set of principles to live by, which when incorporated will expose the myriad of limited beliefs you are operating on. You can use these to get to know yourself better and to be more open to the differences between yourself and other people, giving rise to improved relationships.

Respect the Next Map

With an understanding of the complexity of your own map and how oblivious you may previously have been to how you decide to act, you can see how it would be a simple-minded assumption at any time that you know why the next person behaves the way that they do. This is why two people raised in the same home may well have similarities in their behaviors and belief systems, but they can never be exactly the same. When you respect another individual's map, you acknowledge differences you are and are not aware of. You switch from viewing people from a position of suspicion to one of curiosity and are therefore open to learning instead of dictating.

Behind Every Behavior, There Is a Positive Intention

Our motivations are not the same, and because of this, what pulls us to action will differ. Regardless of what is done, the intention driving it is always positive for the one acting. When someone steals, their intention is to obtain something. Similarly, a lie is often an attempt to protect oneself from something. The liar would do so knowing that if they are caught, they are risking the loss of trust amongst other things, but the motivation behind the lie is greater. This is useful in understanding why you may struggle to change your own behavior. You may thoroughly comprehend that eating junk food every day can lead to a host of health problems, but if you fail to unearth the motivation behind the addiction, you will stop and relapse repeatedly. In the same way, trying to get someone to behave differently without understanding what drives their actions will be a cycle.

If It Isn't Working, Try Something Else

Many people have heard the following definition of insanity: "Insanity: doing the same thing over and over again and expecting different results". We know this, but we are creatures of habit. Another way of looking at this is that nothing changes if nothing changes. If you are looking for results other than what you have experienced so far, you will have to try out another way. Ask yourself how many of your current dissatisfactions and problems are new. NLP practitioners say one of the statements many clients will use for long-term problems is "I have tried everything," only to challenge "everything" and find one avenue explored one way, many times.

We Are Always Communicating

Language is many things; it includes words, gestures, body language, and facial expressions. Even when we are silent, we are communicating something. Bring this into mind going forth and be more intentional about what you are expressing. As you do when creating rapport with someone, pay attention to all the other communication coming from people, other than the words being spoken.

Ecology Is Critical

When evaluating a behavior, it is always important to consider the environment and circumstances under which it takes place. So, if you would like to change a particular behavior, do an assessment of where you are when you generally behave that way and what the trigger is. The same applies when you are trying to gain an understanding of another person's struggle with a behavior that they feel they have no power over. If it is anger, you can first help them to notice that they are not always angry. Believe it or not, no one can be angry all the time. They may not be able to remember all the angry episodes they have had but will most likely be able to recall the last few. There will be a common thread. It could be something like "and then they started taking me for a fool/ they think I'm stupid, so I snapped." If the angered person is verbally insulted this way, they could gain an awareness of the context that brings about their anger; the insulting environment is not conducive for positive behavior. This would be totally different, though, if the angered person is not insulted but habitually arrives at the same meaning for an array of communications, which would imply the need for a content change.

The Meaning of Your Communication Is the Response You Get

You may say something with the intention of a specific interpretation; however, you will only know what is in fact meant to the receiver by how they react or respond. You may be speaking to a client, describing the array of packages you offer, when they abruptly stop you to tell you that their hesitation has nothing to do with a failure to afford. During that moment, you cannot possibly expect to change their map. What you can take in is the understanding that they are sensitive to any perceived assumption of their financial capability. By practicing concise speech and mindful body language, your message can be received as intended.

There Is No Failure—Only Feedback

This presupposition returns to us the allowance that nature already gave us for making mistakes. The older we get, the more we are bound to have more unsuccessful attempts, and we often feel disheartened because we had assumed, as adults, we would just know how to get everything right. If we are going to set real life-altering goals and reach them, we have to get comfortable with all the things we are running from: disappointment, shame, people making fun of us, or even losing some people who we hold onto for the wrong reasons. You might ask yourself what guarantee you have that you will make it; there is none. What you will have gained is increased experience and a movement from where you were before you started.

No One Is Broken

One of the major contrasts between conventional therapy and NLP is that in therapy there are undertones of people being broken. For you to have a true picture of what you are capable of, start by accepting that you are not broken. No one is. Thus far, you have worked perfectly, according to the mental patterns working inside your map, to create the reality you live in. An adaptation or expansion of this map will equally urge you to act differently, and this is how you will see change.

Calibrate Behavior

Studies and surveys prove that a considerable number of people lie to their doctors about their health habits. We do not stop there though. We continue to crack our heads, having tests done to prove what we choose to forget. We believe what we want to believe about ourselves and other people, but more often than not, what we believe is not true. Many people opt to fill in as an "occasional drinker" when the only occasion is getting home after work. So, as you try to find a true picture of who you are right now, pay more attention to how you behave than to the stories you tell yourself. Also, while you interact with other people, believe more of what they are showing you than what they are telling you—they might not be lying intentionally.

You Have What You Need

If you break your goals down into smaller steps, they will cease to look unachievable. You will also be able to see that for the very next step you need to make, you do have what you need. As long as it looks like you do not have what you require for the next step, you are most likely trying to skip ahead. When you adopt the belief that you have what you need, you will start to see every next step. Your subconscious mind holds more information than you are aware of. We get caught up in comparison frequently, where instead of comparing our next step to our own previous location, we are looking at where the next person is in their lives.

Choice Wins

The person who has the most choices will always win. This presupposition encourages you to always have options and to actively look for situations where opportunities do not get closed off. When it begins to feel like you have no choices, your map is shrinking again. Similarly, when you are flexible, your map expands. The one who is willing to take up a job in other countries has more options than the one who confines themselves to one city.

Wholeness Is the Priority

Life can be extremely busy as adults, and much time can go into aspects of life that do not truly matter. People often realize this when they lose a family member or friend to death. You can spend years feuding with people who you could rather be sharing amazing moments with. As you decide which patterns you want to remove and which ones you would like to incorporate, focus on wholeness—the greater good.

Change Your Response, Change Your Map

The inner workings of our patterns are so intricate and interconnected that we are currently unable to capture it all; however, you can change how you behave before it even makes sense to you to do so. If you know that you are tired of fighting with your mother every time you visit her, you can decide to stop fighting, regardless of what she says. This will feel impossible, and you might want to yell right now "You have no idea what she is like!" If you desire to change what's happening, though, you will need to respond differently. Your mind will tell you all sorts of stories when you resist about why you can't allow her to keep talking to you that way. These patterns have thrived up until now and are bound to kick up a fuss, but take back control and act differently.

Presuppositions are not new to you. Our metamodels are largely based on our own presuppositions. In the same light, NLP does not claim that the presuppositions are flawless but are simply assumptions available to replace the old that yield positive results.

Chapter 7: Anchoring

Anchoring is an essential technique in NLP that can be used variably. When you anchor, you link external stimuli with an experience that already exists. How often do you hear a song playing and feel transported back in time to an event, a season, or a period? Sometimes, the words of the song are not even related to the way you will be feeling, but on its own, that song can completely change your mood. That song is an anchor, regardless of what you are doing or how you are feeling. It consistently triggers the same reaction from you.

The concept of anchoring follows Pavlov's theory of Classical Conditioning. Pavlov initially noticed that the dogs he was studying would start salivating whenever they would hear the footsteps of the guard who feeds them. He then decided to start ringing a bell prior to giving the dogs food, and after some time, the dogs started to also salivate just at the sound of the bell without the food. In this case, the bell had become an anchor, triggering the desire to eat in the dogs. Classical conditioning works the same way in humans and can just as easily be switched and assigned to different experiences.

For an anchor to develop, two different aspects need to have happened concurrently a few times. If you follow a routine where you have a cup of tea and then meditate every day, you might be surprised when having your cup of tea that your mind already starts to slip into a meditative state.

Identifying an Anchor in Steps

All of your sensory channels can be used when anchoring.

1. Recall a fully associated experience with the desired resource. It could be a time when you were in love. Many people experience a burst of energy, optimism, and confidence when they are in love, which leads them to have one exhilarating experience after another.

2. Trigger the anchor just before the highest intensity of the emotional state. Using the above example, maybe a certain scent is an anchor, so you intentionally smell it just before you feel the rush you felt when you were in love.

3. Find something to then break away from the experience, like a disruptive question, such as "What time is it?"

4. To ensure that the anchor works, smell the scent again and see if it brings back the rush.

For anchoring to be effective, there are certain key elements the process needs to possess. An anchoring process requires a notable intensity of state. If the experience is more intense, the anchor will be stronger. When you identify an anchor, it has to be intentionally timed to meet the peak of the experience. The anchor should only be associated with that specific state and not used to trigger differing emotional states; doing so would reduce its efficacy. The more times you set the anchor, the more it will mentally stick and have the desired outcome. An operative anchor should have the ability to be fired off the exact same way that it is set.

Most anchors fall under the category of resource anchors, which you set to access a state you find resourceful when you require it, such as an anchor for determination or an anchor for courage if you are prone to shrinking away from what you would like to do. Resource anchors can be stacked to increase intensity. Maybe you would like to feel happy, grateful, and open to life, all at the same time. To stack them, you would recall all of these states, one after the other, and attach them individually to the same anchor. For example, you could decide to anchor them all to a touch of your right ear.

Some people find it unnatural to go from the state they are currently in to their desired one. They would rather go through a few intermediate anchors on their way to the optimum state. This is achievable by chaining anchors. It is a fairly long technique. If you know that every morning you arrive at work feeling bored and defeated, instantly switching to a driven powerhouse would definitely feel like skipping from gear one to five. From the original state, you might prefer to first move to gratitude, optimism, and then inspiration before the desired final anchor. To do this, you would fire off the first anchor, and at its peak, fire off the second anchor. Then, break the first anchor. When the second anchor reaches its peak, fire off the third anchor and break off the second anchor. Continue to follow this pattern until you have arrived at the final anchor, which you will then hold for between five and 15 seconds. For this to be effective, you need to have a deep association with each anchor. When you have successfully chained anchors, you will easily move from defeated to driven.

Sometimes we have unpleasant anchors. The technique of collapsing anchors allows us to take control of negatively associated anchors by reassigning them to a pleasant experience. This is similar to the Swish Pattern. However, when collapsing anchors, the positive recall is an existing memory. The success of collapsing anchors lies in having a positive experience more emotionally charged than the negative one.

Loop Break

When we experience intense highly emotional states, the amygdala and hippocampus work with the body to form a loop reaction. The frontal lobe of the brain moderates behavior, and when a loop reaction occurs, this part of the brain is bypassed. Loop breaks are a way of stopping that loop before the reaction happens. One well-known loop break is to pause and take a few deep breaths. By doing this, you allow the frontal lobe to kick in and rationalize your actions. One way to break a loop is to bring a "comfort thought" to mind. Let's look at an example where you have a colleague who sits on work and only dumps it on you at the last minute, meaning you have to work on a pressured timeline. So, it's going to the end of the month and your colleague starts sending you work, one item after another. Your usual reaction would be to charge to your colleague's desk and lose your cool. To use a comfort thought in this situation, before you get up from your desk you can pause, count to ten and bring to mind the weekend getaway you have been planning. If you are excited about it, your emotional state will shift, and it will not be as easy after this to act irrationally.

Goal Setting

If you haven't already noticed, setting goals is an essential part of NLP. What most people do not notice is how good they already are at achieving their goals. There is a distinct difference between goals and wishes, but people tend to blur this line. Wishes are desires you don't really expect to obtain and are not prepared to do any work toward achieving. Goals, on the other hand, are the ones you intend to become a reality in your life and are equally willing to do what it takes. Every day, you set mini goals. You just do it so well that you have stopped acknowledging them. You set a goal to get the laundry done, another to get to work on time, and another to return your mother's phone call. These are all short-term goals, leading to the medium-term goals of having clean clothes, earning a salary, and maintaining important relationships. The long-term goal encompassing all of this is to survive. When you attempt to be intentional about setting your goals, suddenly the steps you take to go from desire to actualization can seem mystical when they are in fact very simple.

Step One: What Do You Want?

Start by deciding what it is you want to achieve. Give particular attention to the word "you." You have been told what the indicators of success are verbally or by watching how society standardizes things. But what does success mean for you? The answer to this question is what each individual goal needs to reflect.

Step Two: Be Specific

If we refer again to the example of setting a goal to get to work on time, automatically the next thing you would do is have a target time, which makes your goal specific. Now going back to our VAKOG types. When you put details on your goal, add the ones that match your strongest senses. Let's assume your goal is to buy a car—a visual person would do well for themselves to put more focus into what the car will look like, while an auditory person will do better to focus on the functions.

Step Three: Determine Your Location

Imagine trying to get somewhere you have never been, without any idea of where you currently are. It could make your journey a lot longer, and the likelihood of succeeding would be greatly reduced. Once you have figured out where you are, make it clear to yourself why you are unsatisfied with it. If your goal is to buy a big house, you might assess your current location and find that you are living in a small house, and it makes you unhappy because you feel cramped up and restricted from buying other things you would like to. You want the big house because it will give you ample space for your family and other purchases.

Step Four: Resonance

All the other goals you achieve without a thought resonate with who you are. If you struggle to reach a goal, most likely there is some internal resistance. Using the same example of the big house, if there is a part of you that holds a belief that you should continue to live in the neighborhood you do, this could be causing a lack of resonance if you know you cannot build a big house in that area. Working through your conflicting beliefs releases the parts of your mind that are resisting, allowing them to align with your desires.

Step Five: Obstacles

Artists will tell you that one of the hurdles they frequently face is finishing the works they have started. The fact that they will leave it and start a different piece implies that they do not run out of creativity, but what does happen sometimes is that a part of them is scared of seeing it through to completion and putting it out into the world for scrutiny. The fear, therefore, stops the goal of creating a work of art by causing a sudden disconnection to the work. The fear is the obstacle causing the disconnection to the work. Once you have found the obstacles standing in your way, you can use a suitable NLP technique to change the operating pattern.

Step Six: Immediate Action

One of the top excuses for not exercising is not having the money to pay for a gym membership. This excuse leads people to procrastinate for months that turn into years. When you set goals, it is important to find immediate steps you can start taking toward them. Your mind may initially struggle to prioritize what has never been given precedence, but you will find that the more you exercise, if going to the gym is something you truly want, your mind will organize itself to avail the money for a membership. By putting it off for a more convenient time, you reinforce to your mind how unimportant the goal is.

Step Seven: Visualization

Visualization is a powerful technique to add to your goal setting because it makes use of your senses. Previously, it was believed that if you cannot visualize something using your sense of (inner) sight, you will struggle to see it manifest; however, with the understanding that we have different strengths to our sensations, this visualization encourages prioritizing your strongest senses. One person may not find it easy to use their imagination to visualize a partner they dream of having, but it will come more naturally for them to connect to how their dream partner would feel. Others might be able to hear music or the voice this person would have. If you are able to engage all of your senses, this will provide a heightened experience. The more detailed your visualization is, the stronger your sensations will be. Your mind will strive to achieve this bliss, and this is how the path will form.

Conclusion

If you do not take anything else out of this book, take the fact that whatever way you have been seeing the world has been unique to you. The information and techniques in this book are aimed at expanding your view and making it more accommodative of other perspectives. There is a map you have been running on for this long, and regardless of how much you have been exposed to, it will serve you better to always be aware that there is more to learn. Education has provided us with an illusion that you can go from one level to the next until you get to a perceived place of being "all-knowing." The intention of education, which we have missed, is to open our minds to an expanse of information, rather than to close us within an idea that we can possibly ever know it all. NLP is a conditioning of the mind, allowing and encouraging us to approach life with curiosity.

By understanding the unique way you see the world and the senses you prioritize, you can take charge of how your story will play out. Thus far, we have adhered to a system of good, better, and best as opposed to acknowledging that there is difference, variability, and still nuance. Instead of allowing learned patterns to control us, NLP gives us the opportunity to actually create a life with our signature on it. Language is something we have taken for granted, yet it is the very thing that binds us to all of life's phenomena. We communicate through language and label what we experience the same way. Despite the different languages we speak, we have still managed to break the barriers, because language is more than words. Language is how you make sense of your experiences, and even the oldest texts in the world tell us that the tongue holds the power of life and death. What does your tongue tell you, and what does it lead you toward?

The section on metamodels brings to light the way our speech continues to reinforce certain patterns, rendering us stuck in stories we want to change. Understanding meta programs gives us a chance to see that there is a filter we habitually carry that will paint everything the same color. With awareness, equally, comes the opportunity and responsibility in yourself to choose better. The increased cognition that we do not actually see life as it is makes us more alert and compassionate to the operating filters around us. Is it possible that the way you have been interpreting someone's behavior is not actually what they are communicating?

There are many solutions out there to changing one area of our lives or the other. By incorporating the NLP techniques, you can take control of your life as a whole, because the only aspect controlling you so far is your mind and the stories it has held onto for the longest time. That hardly makes the mind bad. On the contrary, it works efficiently to protect you, but if you continued to stop a baby whenever they tried to get up, they would be convinced that they cannot walk.

Now that you understand that you find what you go out looking for in this world, the presuppositions provide a preferential perspective known to have yielded substantial results. You will have found that NLP works with techniques that the mind has already been using but fine-tunes them to maximize your abilities. Anchoring, as explained, is one of these examples, being the reason why we have powerful memories and phobias, meant to protect us. But this same technique can be used to evoke the states of mind we excel on. Goal setting, whether intentional or simply by living, will always be part of human existence.

When NLP was created, the idea was to find how successful people's mindsets and behavior differed from everyone else's, unearthing considerable distinctions. Following this, people have tried to copy the lifestyles of successful people, falling short because the filters through which they see the world are entirely different. Isn't it so that you will read of a prominent figure who has gone broke, but in no time, they are back to living a lavish life? For them, broke is not an option, and their broke is not the same as yours: their filter versus yours.

NLP does not invalidate our stories and experiences but rather acknowledges the power of a story. We hold on to stories long after their existence, refusing to let them die, until we pass them on genetically. If we are going to hold onto stories, it would make the most sense to choose the ones that build us. Now you are aware of the limitations of your patterns, and you have been given the keys. You have what you need, you have a choice, and you can work perfectly to achieve whatever you decide to go after.

www.ingramcontent.com/pod-product-compliance
Lightning Source LLC
LaVergne TN
LVHW021736060526
838200LV00052B/3310